FUNDS TO PURCHASE
THIS BOOK WERE
PROVIDED BY A
40TH ANNIVERSARY GRANT
FROM THE
FOELLINGER FOUNDATION.

Through the Eyes of CHILDREN

TANZANIA

Connie Bickman

Published by Abdo & Daughters, 4940 Viking Drive, Suite 622, Edina, Minnesota 55435.

Copyright © 1996 by Abdo Consulting Group, Inc., Pentagon Tower, P.O. Box 36036, Minneapolis, Minnesota 55435 USA. International copyrights reserved in all countries. No part of this book may be reproduced in any form without written permission from the publisher.

Printed in the United States.

Cover Photo credit: Connie Bickman
Interior Photo credits: Connie Bickman

Edited by Julie Berg

LIBRARY OF CONGRESS CATALOGING-IN-PUBLICATION DATA

Bickman, Connie
    Children of Tanzania / Connie Bickman.
      p. cm. -- (Through the eyes of children)
    Includes Index.
    Summary: Introduces the people, food, clothing, and daily life of Tanzania.

    ISBN 1-56239-547-5
    1. Tanzania--Social life and customs-- Juvenile Literature. 2. Children--Tanzania--Social life and customs--Juvenile literature. [1. Tanzania --Social life and customs.] I. Title. II. Series.
    DT442.5.B5 1996
    967.8--dc20   95-39543
                                         CIP
                                         AC

Contents

Welcome to Tanzania!

The name Tanzania came from the uniting of two countries.
These countries were Tanganyika and Zanzibar.
They united in 1964, making one country, Tanzania. It is south of the equator, the largest country in East Africa. It is also the poorest.

The mainland of Tanzania is located on the east coast of Africa.
Off the coast are the Indian Ocean Islands of Zanzibar and other small coral islands.
Tanzania's borders are Kenya, Uganda, Rwanda, Burundi, and Zaire.
Other border countries are Zambia, Malawi and Mozambique.
The Great Rift Valley runs through the eastern length of Africa.
It is a series of faultlines or gashes in the earth's surface.
Many years ago they helped form large lakes, volcanic valleys, plateaus, and high mountains.

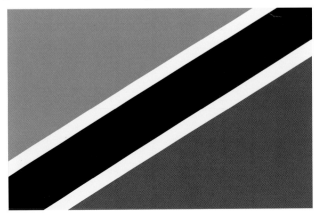

The flag of Tanzania.

Lake Tanganyika, Victoria Lake, and Lake Malawi are some of the country's beautiful lakes.

The bottom of Lake Tanganyika is the deepest point on the African continent.

It is also the longest freshwater lake in the world, 419 miles (674 km) long.

Lake Victoria is one of the world's largest freshwater lakes, 26,828 square miles (43,166 square km).

The Nile River, the longest river in the world, flows north from Lake Victoria.

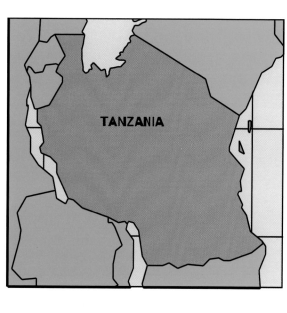

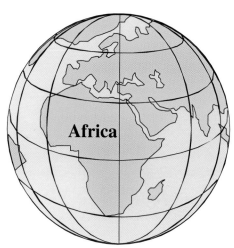

Pictures in caves and on rocks are called petroglyphs. They are a record of the history of the land, drawn by tribesmen many years ago.

Many of them are of animals they hunted and pictures showing their way of life.

The land of Tanzania can be very different from border to border.

There are banana and coconut trees and long sandy beaches on the coast.

The countryside has tall snow-covered mountains, dry riverbeds, and rocky hills.

Dry woodland called miombo and huge baobab trees grow inland.

There are twelve National Parks and Game Reserves. Olduvai Gorge has footprints that are believed to be four million years old!

Selous Game Reserve is the largest animal reserve in all of Africa.

The Serengeti Plain is vast bush country where wild animals live.

The Ngorongoro Crater is an ancient volcano filled with wildlife.

Tanzania is a country with wide open spaces and beautiful landscapes.

Meet the Children

"Jambo!"
That is a word of greeting in Swahili.
Swahili is also called Kiswahili.
Swahili uses the same alphabet as English.
Swahili and English are the national languages of
Tanzania.
Many children also speak other ethnic languages,
depending on what region of the country they live in.

There are 120 different ethnic groups and cultures in
Tanzania.
Most of the people in Tanzania (95 percent) are black
Africans from Bantu origin.
Major groups are Sukuma, Maasai, Nyamwezi, Chaga,
Hehe, Bena, Makonde, and Haya.
The earliest hunter-gatherer people are the San
(Bushman) and Khoikhoi (Hottentot).
Shirazi, Muslim settlers, live along the Zanzibar coast.

What Do They Eat?

Rice, papayas, wheat, sweet potatoes, corn, sugar cane, and bananas are very important foods.
The fruit is used for eating, the stems are fed to cows and the leaves are used for thatching roofs.
Spices, tobacco, tea and coffee are also local products.

The basic food is a stiff porridge made from cornmeal flour.
It is called ugali.

Fresh vegetables are tomatos, cabbage, cauliflower, green beans, potatoes, and onions.
In some areas vegetables are not eaten regularly and many tribes do not eat meat.

Spicy rice and meat dishes are popular along the coast and in Zanzibar.
The Maasai tribe's diet is mostly cows' milk mixed with blood.

What Do They Wear?

Many children in Tanzania wear T-shirts, jeans, and dresses just like you do.
Some tribes wear traditional clothing.
A khanga is fabric used as a wrap-around skirt, scarf, or shawl.
It is usually very colorful and worn in most parts of the country.

Muslim men wear a flowing white robe called a kanzu and a hat called a kofia.

Muslim women wear a black dress with a hood called a buibui.

The Maasai wear beaded collars, earrings, and jewelry. They also wear stacks of bracelets on their ankles and wrists.

In the cities people wear Western-style clothing, like jeans or dresses.
When Maasai or other tribal people go to the city they also wear Western-style clothing.

Where Do They Live?

Most of the people of Tanzania live in small villages.
Many of them do not have running water or electricity.
Some of their houses are built of cow dung and straw.
The insides have dirt floors, a fire pit, and a place to
sleep.
The family spends most of their time outside.

Houses are made from materials found on the land. That would be banana or palm leaves, straw or mud. Some houses are made from bricks and stones with tin roofs. Most of the houses in small villages are cement with open windows.

There are also beautiful modern houses in the countryside. They are usually owned by plantation farmers.

Getting Around

There are many airports and landing strips in Tanzania.
Some of these landing strips carry people and supplies into the bush.
Airplanes are used to bring tourists in for safari.
They are also used for emergency medical carriers for The Flying Doctors.
Sailboats called dhows have been used on the coast for centuries.
They are used to carry people and supplies.

Railroads, buses, jeeps, and cars are used in the more urban areas.

For most people bicycles are the main source of transportation.

Riding donkeys and wooden oxen carts are other ways of getting around.

School is Fun!

Children begin shule (school) when they are seven years old.

School is provided free by the government.

Most of the villages build their own schools.

These children are at recess from their classroom in Arusha.

Their school is surrounded by cornfields and agricultural land.

Children attend secondary school when they are 14.

Then they can go on to trade schools or colleges.

Swahili is the main language, but English is also taught.

They also learn history, geography, mathematics, health, physical education, and science.

How Do They Work?

Herding goats and cattle is a job for many young boys.
In the bush there is not always a lot of food to eat so
they have to find new ground often.
It is a hot and dusty job.
Children also have to help collect firewood and water
and help with chores.

Hauling bundles of coffee beans on a bicycle can take
good balance.
Sometimes children help on coffee, cotton, or
sugarcane plantations.
Ninety percent of the land is cultivated on small farms.
On the coast and in the larger lakes fishing is a job
that keeps older children busy.

Animals

Millions of animals live in the wilds of Tanzania.
Maasai giraffe, elephants, lions, zebra, cape buffalo, rhinoceros, and hippopotumus.
Kudu, gazelle, crocodile, ostrich, gazelle, topi, eland, monkeys, and wildebeest.
There are also many kinds of colorful birds like flamingos and secretary birds.
People come to Tanzania to go on safari to look at these beautiful birds and animals.
The animals are wild and you have to be very careful and obey all the rules of the bush.
Africa is a very exciting land.

The Land

The bush and grasslands of the Maasai steppe make up most of the central region.
The fertile valley of the Ngorongoro Crater makes it a permanent home for some Maasai tribes.
The crater is 11 miles (18 km) across and has over 25,000 animals living in it!

Mount Kilimanjaro is Africa's highest point at 19,340 feet (5,895 meters).
It is in the upper section of the Northern Highlands.
It is only three degrees south of the equator.
It is near the town of Arusha.

The Serengeti Plains is a huge wildlife reserve.
There are rules for preserving the land and the
animals that live there.
Millions of wild animals roam the vast lands of Africa.
There are many other game reserves that try to keep
these animals safe.

Almost half the land is covered with forests.
Green meadows, pastures, and wooded grasslands
spread throughout the country.
Mangrove forests are found on the coast.
In some areas beautiful flowers are grown, including
large red poinsettias.

What are Traditions?

Some tribes have celebrations for young girls.
The girls wear rings on all their fingers and toes.
They have their hair beaded and special ceremonies take place.
It is a tradition.

In some tribes young boys celebrate with special headdresses. They are made from bird feathers, bark, and other things found in the bush. Wearing these headresses is a special tradition.

Many years ago there was a tradition at weddings and celebrations.
Natives would gather around a big rock called "Gong Rock."
They would take small rocks in their hands and pound dents in Gong Rock.
Each dent would make a special sound.
The gases in the rock made different tones.
Gong Rock was like playing a musical instrument.
It made the music for traditional celebrations.

Children are the Same

It is fun to see how children in other countries live.
Children may play and go to school and have families
just like you.
They may work, travel, and dress differently than you.
One thing is always the same.
That is a smile.
If you smile at other children, they will smile back.
That is how you make new friends.
It is fun to have new friends all over the world!

Glossary

Arusha (ah-RU-shah) - a city where many safaris begin.
Bantu (BAN-too) - tribal laguage.
Baobab (BAY-o-bab) - gigantic trees that are used for medicine, food, and building materials.
Bena (BE-na) - ethnic tribe.
Buibui (BUI-bui) - black hooded dress worn by Muslims.
Burundi (bur-UN-di) - northwest border to Tanzania.
Chaga (CHA-ga) - ethnic group that lives on the southern slope of Mt. Kilimanjaro.
Dar es Salaam (dar es sal-AM) - the former capital of Tanzania.
Dhows (dows) - ancient sailboats.
Dodoma (DO-do-ma) - the new capital of Tanzania.
Haya (HAY-ah) - ethnic tribe.
Hehe (He-he) - ethnic tribe.
Jambo (JAWM-bo) - Swahili for hello or greetings.
Kanzu (KHAN-zoo) - white flowing robes worn by Muslims.
Kenya (KEEN-yah) - northern border of Tanzania.
Khanga (KHAN-gah) - colorful fabric worn as a skirt, shawl, or scarf.
Khoikhoi (KOY-koy) - ethnic tribe, also known as Hottentot.
Kiswahili (ki-swa-HE-li) - another name for Swahili.
Kofia (KO-fia) - Muslim hat.
Maasai (MAA-si) - ethnic tribe living in the northern area. Known as warriors, they are usually nomadic cattlemen.
Makonde (ma-KON-de) - ethnic tribe known for ebony wood sculptures.

Malawi (ma-LA-wee) - southern border to Tanzania.
Miombo (mi-OM-bo) - areas of dry woodland.
Mount Kilimanjaro (kil-i-man-JAR-o) - highest mountain in Africa—19,340 feet (5,895 m).
Mozambique (mo-zam-BEEK) - southern border to Tanzania.
Ngorongoro Crater (n-GORO-goro) - an 11-mile (18 km) natural volcanic crater where wildlife live.
Nyamwezi (ni-am-WE-ze) - ethnic tribe.
Olduvai Gorge (OL-du-vai) - area where four-million-year-old footprints have been found.
Rwanda (row-WAN-dah) - northwest border of Tanzania.
San - a bushman tribe.
Selous Game Reserve (SE-lous) - the largest animal reserve in Africa.
Serengeti (ser-en-GET-ti) - a National Wildlife reserve.
Shiruzi (shir-U-zl) - descendants of early Persian Muslim settlers.
Shule (SHOOL) - Swahili for school.
Sukuma (sue-KUM-ah) - ethnic tribe. Sukuma means "people to the north." Sukuma are traditional snake charmers.
Swahili (Swa-HE-lee) - official language of Tanzania.
Tanganyika (tang-gan-KNEE-kaw) - the deepest point in Africa. The longest freshwater lake in the world.
Ugali (u-GAHL-li) - stiff porridge made from corn meal flour.
Uganda (you-GAN-dah) - northwest border of Tanzania.
Zaire (zaa-EAR) - western border of Tanzania.
Zambia (ZAM-bee-ah) - southern border of Tanzania.
Zanzibar (ZAN-zi-bar) - the islands off the coast of Tanzania.

Index

31

About the Author/Photographer

Connie Bickman is a photojournalist whose photography has won regional and international awards.

She is retired from a ten-year newspaper career and currently owns her own portrait studio and art gallery. She also is an active freelance photographer and writer who travels the far corners of the world to photograph native cultures.

Connie is a member of the National Press Association and the Minnesota Newspaper Photographers Association.